Tomáš Míček

ANDALUSIAN HORSES

Text by
Dr. Hans-Jörg Schrenk

SUNBURST BOOKS

Poseido, one of the stallions from the Terry Stud, enjoys his freedom on the Atlantic coast, west of Puerto de Santa Maria.

"Caballo de Pura Raza Espanola" - horse of pure Spanish breed - this is the official description of the Spanish horses which most people know by the name of Andalusian. All horse-lovers are enchanted by the features of the Andalusians - their balletic elegance, their agility, their high-stepping gait and their compact body with its luxurious, long mane and strong neck. The image of fiery stallions with plaited, decorated manes stepping out in piaffe and pirouette, or as part of a smart carriage team presents an unforgettable picture. However these horses are at their most beautiful when they are untouched by human hand, galloping free in the meadow or along the beaches of the Spanish Atlantic coast. Tomáš Míček has captured these moments on film, visiting the most famous Spanish studs to provide the impressive photos in this book.

Habanero, another stallion from the Terry Stud, profiled against the setting sun on the beach of Vista Hermosa.

The dark grey stallion, Genil, from Don Miguel Cárdenas' stud, letting off steam amongst the dunes on the Atlantic coast.

Overleaf: In the hazy light of the setting sun the herd of mares from Don Miguel Cárdenas' stud head home. The manes of the mares are usually clipped in Spain - only the stallions are allowed to display the full splendour of their long manes.

*The herd of mares from the Terry Stud up in the hills where the meadows
are covered with grass and herbs in the early summer - later the land
becomes dry and parched by the blazing Andalusian sun.*

The stallion, Habanero, pursuing a mare.

The history of the Andalusian horses begins before the birth of Christ. As long ago as 200 BC, at the time of the Roman conquests in and around Spain, Roman writers reported on the superb horses of Andalusia, which were superior to all other breeds in the Roman Empire. Later, the Moorish conquerors, who ruled over Spain for about 700 years, also held these horses in high esteem. The Moors certainly cross-bred the native Spanish horses with their own Arab and Berber breeds, although investigations by equine experts indicate that this did not have a very strong influence on the Andalusians. After the Moors were driven from Spain in the 15th century, the noble Spanish horse experienced a period of great popularity. All the monarchs and courts of Europe considered the Andalusians to be the best parade and haute école horses.

This mare is keeping watch over her foal, which is just a few hours old, in the meadows of Finca Encinar de Vicos, owned by Don Diego Díez Gutierrez.

The Andalusian had a great influence on almost all other European horse breeds. The Lipizzaner, Kladruber, Friesian, Neapolitan and Fredericksborg breeds in particular are directly descended from the Andalusian. Furthermore, many Andalusians were taken to the New World in America following numerous Spanish conquests there, and consequently many Central, South and North American horses can be traced back to this Spanish breed. When it became fashionable in Spain to cross heavier, foreign horses with the Andalusians, the order of Carthusian monks opposed this trend, and it is thanks to them that the ancient, pure line of the Andalusians was preserved. The monks were resistant to any outside influences and trends and continued with their pure breeding policy at their large studs in Seville and Cordoba. All of today's noble horses of pure Spanish breed can be traced back to these Carthusian studs, which were later taken over by private breeders. Today pure-bred Andalusians are much in demand and bred throughout the world.

This Spanish-Anglo-Arab foal observes his surroundings with interest on the Finca Encinar de Vicos. The crossing of Andalusians with English and Arab thoroughbreds is intended to bring out those features of each breed which are best suited to riding, to produce the best possible sporting horse.

Vasallo, one of Don Miguel Cárdenas' stallions in Ecija.

The main Andalusian breeding areas are in southern Spain in the region of Andalusia itself, particularly in the provinces of Cadiz, Seville and Cordoba. There are also studs along the Portuguese border, as well as in Castille and Catalonia and on the Balearic islands. The number of studs outside Spain is also on the increase. Andalusians are popular throughout the world for their beauty, charm and performance. There are large studs in America and Australia, and in Germany there is an association of friends and breeders of horses of pure Spanish breed, which aims to breed Andalusians according to the aims and regulations of the Spanish studbook.

It looks as if Vasallo has got wind of an interesting smell - he throws up his head and flares his nostrils to detect the source.

One of the distinctive features of all the horses of pure Spanish breed is their silky, flowing mane.

In spring and early summer the fields of Andalusia are covered in a stunning, colourful carpet of wild flowers. A grey stallion from the Terry Stud surrounded by yellow flowers.

The breeding of Andalusians is monitored by the Spanish government in Madrid, which also has its own military stud at Jerez de la Frontera. The government authorities are responsible for the stud book. The conditions for entry into the stud book are very strict: to be awarded a certificate, a foal must be passed by a government commission, and all three year olds have to be re-presented to this commission, where they are judged according to appearance, gait and temperament. Any horse which does not meet the criteria of this examination cannot be registered or used for stud.

An unusual sight: a black Andalusian stallion. Grey is the most common colour amongst the pure-bred Spanish horses, followed by bay. Black is quite uncommon, and chestnut or piebald horses are not considered to be pure-bred and therefore are excluded from the studbook.

The breeding standards for horses of pure Spanish breed describes the Andalusian as a medium-sized horse, with a straight or slightly convex profile and a lively gait with high knee action. The head should be of medium length with refined features, well-set ears, a broad, flat or slightly curved forehead and large, expressive eyes. The neck should also be of medium length and slightly curved, with a thick and silky mane. Prominent withers are specified, as well as a broad chest, sloping, well-muscled shoulders, a short, horizontal back and round, sloping quarters with a low-set tail, which is carried close to the body. Both fore and hind legs should be straight. About 50% of Andalusians are grey. Bay and black horses are also quite common, and occasionally one sees chestnuts and piebalds, which are not allowed to be listed in the stud book, as these colours are considered to be atypical for the breed.

Poseido stands like a statue in a sea of poppies.

The temperament of the Andalusian is another plus point, alongside its outstanding beauty and elegant movement. Despite the rather fiery impression which it presents, this breed is quite docile and affectionate towards people. Even handling stallions - in Spain male horses are not usually castrated - does not normally present any problems. The Andalusians are good-natured, intelligent and quick to learn, and are always keen to do whatever their rider asks, which is why they are much in demand in haute école.

Poseido again on the Terry Stud. Here, away from people, amongst the trees, the horse's enjoyment in galloping free is clear to see.

*A mock fight between two young stallions at Finca El Hornillo in Seville,
owned by Don Juan Manuel de Urquijo.*

Contrary to appearances, this is just a friendly fight, as indicated by the fact that the horses' ears are pointing forwards.

In Spain there are two different styles of riding, both of which are widespread. Many of the pure-bred Spanish horses are trained in both of these styles. In the Doma Vaquera riding style of the Spanish cattle herders and bullfighters, curb reins and a comfortable, deep saddle are used. The Doma Vaquera style relies very much on the transfer of weight to balance the rider, and the reins are held in the left hand, leaving the right free to deal with the cattle.

However the Andalusian is the true master of the "Alta Escuela" - the classical Spanish riding school. Here these horses demonstrate their natural talent for the haute école figures such as *passage*, *piaffe* and the so-called "Spanish trot," which was actually named after the Andalusian.

Their intelligence and capacity to learn is reflected in the ease with which these horses familiarise themselves with these lessons, with minimal intervention from the teacher. Like their "sons," the Lipizzaners at the Spanish Riding School in Vienna, the Andalusians are much admired for their ability to perform complex movements on a lunge rein without a rider.

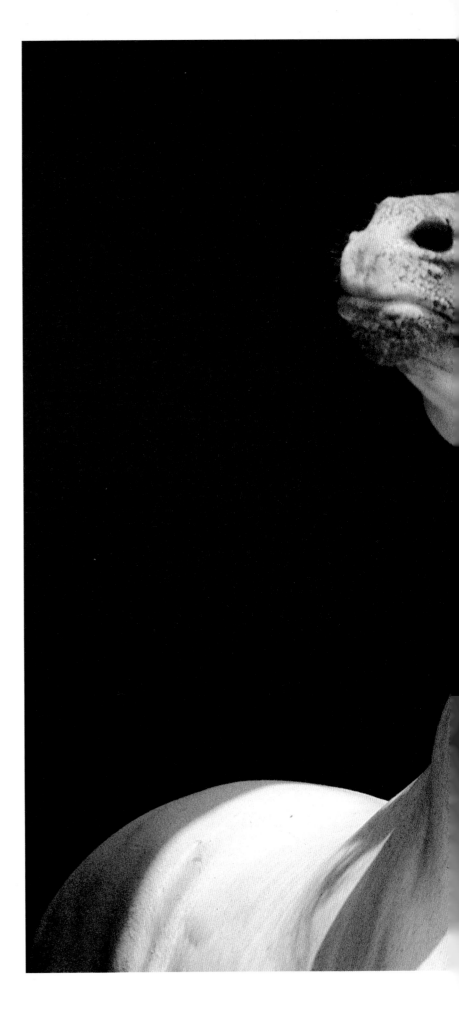

Barquillero, a stud stallion owned by the Diosdado family, at Finca El Portal in Jerez de la Frontera, showing off the full beauty of his thick mane as he tosses his head.

A young colt full of the joys of life at Finca Encinar de Vicos, owned by Don Diego Díez Gutierrez, who also breeds Spanish-Anglo-Arabs.

This little chestnut foal observes his surroundings curiously, but feels safer close to his mother's side. When he's a few weeks older he'll risk some excursions further afield.

Two Spanish-Anglo-
Arab mares with their
foals at the Hacienda
Buendía de Bucare close
to Seville.

A mare with her foal which is only about 3 hours old in the Finca Monanies meadows of the Terry Stud.

The little foal is already taking a keen interst in his surroundings. He does not even appear to be frightened by the photographer and remains calmly stretched out on his side.

The many positive characteristics of the Andalusians make them ideal riding horses, although they are more suitable for those who are looking for an intelligent horse for recreational riding or dressage, rather than a horse for competitive sporting activities. Andalusians are also relatively easy and low-cost animals to keep, as a result of their tough upbringing in their native country and their frugal food requirements.

The grey stallion, Vasallo, in the meadows of Finca el Corrin, owned by Don Miguel Cárdenas.

The stallion, Poseido, amidst the brightly coloured flowers of the Spanish spring at the Terry Stud. He enjoys the smell of the fresh green grass, but the direction of his eyes and ears shows that he is still paying close attention to what's going on in his surroundings.

He watches the approaching photographer closely, but isn't really disturbed by him.

On the Hazienda Lerena, west of Seville, Francisco Lazo Díaz de Castaños breeds the coveted bay Andalusians.

*In the picture on the facing page the stallion makes the most of his freedom
in the sun drenched meadows of the hacienda.*

Bay Andalusians are also bred in the vicinity of Jerez de la Frontera at the Finca Los Canos Aduza, owned by Antonio and Cristobal Diosdado. This stallion eyes the camera watchfully.